ZAKYNTHOS

TOURIST GUIDE • USEFUL INFORMATION • MAP

- DESCRIPTION OF THE TOWN
- TOURS • PLACES OF INTEREST
- LIST OF HOTELS AND CAMPING SITES

GREEK TEXTS: HELENE PALASKA – PAPASTATHI

© ADAM EDITIONS, 275 MESOGION AVE., 152 31 ATHENS
TEL.: (01) 6721801-3, 6470072,TLX: 214223 ADAM GR., FAX: (01) 6725015

CONTENTS

ZAKYNTHOS

The island's rich vegetation and serene natural environment, its peaceful landscape unruffled by the rocky protuberances of the mountains which instead merely add variety, an innate feeling of langour that seems to pervade every corner of the island whether by the sea or up in the mountains - all these contribute to creating an illusion of paradise. If you were to add all these elements together, then you would be bound to agree that yes, Zakynthos is a paradise! It may not have so strong an element of primitivism, but there is no doubt that it is a latter-day paradise on earth.

The third largest of the Ionian Islands, Zakynthos lies 8.5 miles to the south of Kephallonia with its most northerly point, Schinari, opposite Mouda at the southern tip of Kephallonia. It is roughly 125 kilometres in length, and covers an area of 410 square kilometres.

To the east, at a distance of approximately 9.5 miles, is the coast of the Peloponnese to which the island is linked by a frequent ferry service (the trip from Kyllini to Zakynthos takes about an hour and a half). The narrowest gap between the island and the mainland is between Trypiti in the Peloponnese and Kryoneri on Zakynthos.

The terrain is varied; there are plains in the eastern part which merge gently into peaceful bays and golden beaches, while the western side of the island is mountainous with steep

Above:
The little port of Aghios Nikolaos.

Left:
The abrupt coasts of the island inspire a feeling of awe.

11

cliffs along its coastline. Although the mountains are not particularly high, they occupy a fair portion of the island. The highest is Mount Vrachionas (758 metres), and other mountains of note are Kaki Rachi (680 metres), Mount Atheras (583 metres) and Mount Skopos (483 metres), with some lower ones that together form a small plateau.

The main bays are at Laganas, in the south, which has a fantastic sandy beach that stretches for 90 kilometres, Tsilivi, Alykes, and Schiza. The most important promontories are those at Schinari and Marathia, at the island's most northerly and southerly points respectively; Keri in the south-west, Yeraki on the north-east coast of the island, and Kryoneri which lies to the north of the town of Zakynthos.

Laganas Bay encompasses the rocky and uninhabited islets of Marathonisi, Agios Sostis and Pelouzo, with the Strofades islands (which belong administratively to the prefecture of Zakynthos) lying about 75 km. to the south.

Zakynthos has many underground streams which are fed by a number of wells and springs; the island is therefore blessed with an ample water supply, which together with its fertile soil guarantees a plentiful supply of agricultural produce. The island's main products are oil, grapes, wine, citrus fruits, potatoes and onions, and upland pastures ensure a considerable amount of animal-rearing.

From a geological viewpoint the island is of great interest. Geologists believe that in the distant past Zakynthos was part of a submarine plate which was pushed up as a result of strong tremors to form an island. The major geological realignments in this marine region resulted in the creation of lots of little islets, reefs and underwater shelves. They also caused the opening of a huge underwater fault known as "The Well of Inousses" to the southeast of Zakynthos, where the Mediterranean is at its deepest (approx. 4,500 metres).

Left, above: Laganas.

Below: Tsilivi.

As a result of the intense geological activity in the region some remarkable caves were formed on the island, both on land and in the sea. Some of these are extremely interesting and there is public access to many of them.

The soil of Zakynthos contains gypsum, sulphur and hydrocarbons. In the southern part of the island, near Keri, bituminous water gushes out of the ground, but the drilling of boreholes in the area in search of oil has proved fruitless.

The climate of the island is mild, with gentle winters and cool summers. The plentiful rainfall, in contrast to the rare occurrence of snow, favours the growth of vegetation and ensures considerable water reserves, which is why the island is so green.

Below: The beach at Alykes.

Right: Porto Zorro.

Apart from the olive groves and vineyards, orchards full of citrus trees and every other kind of fruit, areas of garden produce and grain,

much of the island is forested and on some of the beaches trees grow right down to the water's edge. The island's rich vegetation and serene natural environment, its peaceful landscape unruffled by the rocky protuberances of the mountains which instead merely add variety, an innate feeling of langour that seems to pervade every corner of the island whether by the sea or up in the mountains - all these contribute to creating an illusion of paradise. If you were to add all these elements together, then you would be bound to agree that yes, Zakynthos is a paradise! It may not have so strong an element of primitivism, but there is no doubt that it is a latter-day paradise on earth.

Above:
The cosmopolitan beach of Laganas and the islet of Aghios Sostis.

Left:
Tsilivi.

Above:
Zakynthian
handwork.

Right:
Old stone
well.

The people of Zakynthos are optimistic, cheerful, friendly and talkative. They are known for their placidity and their politeness, but also for their love of the Arts and Literature. This particular aspect of the Zakynthian personality has made a sizeable contribution to its exceptional cultural record as a whole. It is no mere coincidence that such a small place has given so much, both qualitatively and quantitatively, to the Arts and Letters of modern Greece.

An intrinsic aptitude, certain inherent inclinations, a natural feeling for culture and the special circumstances that prevail in the Ionian Islands overall provided the right conditions for the pursuit of scholarly excellence by a large section of the island's population. The pursuit became creation, and the creation became Art or the appreciation of Art.

The very nature of the island, on the other hand, the magic qualities of the scenery and the peaceful succession of the seasons have injected the people with a sense of poetry, a love of life and nature.

The people of Zakynthos are extremely attached to their native island home; they are concerned about its progress and are ready to make an active contribution wherever and whenever they are needed. They were present at all the major battles, even those against the elements of Nature; they clung on fiercely to even the faintest and most fragile of hopes, and succeeded in turning them into reality, emerging from the struggle bold, strong and full of self-assurance.

An open-minded people with modern ideas and cosmopolitan attitudes, they are noted for their natural and effortless courtesy, particularly towards guests.

Since the days of Venetian rule the Zakynthian has always had a European air about him, although this does not mean that he looks down on anything that is authentic and rooted in local tradition. He respects the manners and customs of his island, and enters wholeheartedly into the merry-making on feast-days and other celebrations.

Situated as it is between East and West, the island was subjected to a number of foreign influences which it wisely and selectively turned to good advantage. It did not succumb to the temptation of facile imitation; rather each new element adopted was absorbed after a long and painful process and embraced by the island's own special characteristics, having been

passed through a kind of "Zakynthian filter". The Zakynthian dialect is melodious and easy on the ear. The musical timbre of the voice, the torrent of words (many of which have Italian roots), the sing-song lilt of the voices, the gestures tinged with a natural theatricality, all contribute to a lively and expressive picture of the people of Zakynthos.

In former times many of the inhabitants of the island made a living from agriculture, animal-rearing and fishing, while others were skilled craftsmen such as builders, blacksmiths and carpenters. As the soil is fertile and yields rich crops, few people left the island to seek their fortune in the major Greek cities or overseas. There was, however, a wave of emigration from Zakynthos in the wake of the 1953 earthquakes. Nowadays the islanders' main occupation is tourism and related activities. The burgeoning tourist industry, which began in a modest way during the 1960's and developed steadily over the last three decades, has brought economic prosperity to Zakynthos.

Above:
St. Mark's square.

Left:
Zakynthos, the port.

27

With the continuously growing demand for tourist accommodation in recent years, there has been a tremendous increase in building activity. The building industry and related trades are therefore flourishing. A large number of tourist facilities have sprung up in the town of Zakynthos and the nearby summer resorts. At the same time, however, conscious efforts are being made to preserve the island's traditional architectural style and protect the environment.

More and more visitors are attracted by the natural beauty of the island, its pleasant and healthy climate, cool greenery, crystal-clear sea and endless sandy beaches, and by the warmth of its people.

Below: Aghios Nikolaos.

The Museum of Dionysios Solomos and Eminent Zakynthians, on the historic square of St. Mark.

Right: Ruins beside Argassi.

Because of its geographic location Zakynthos was the target of countless forays, and consequently the island's history amounts to an enumeration of the most significant of these attacks and the efforts by the islanders to fend them off. The island rose up out of the depths of the Ionian Sea like a sea nymph, or so experts believe, but the history of her far-distant past remains uncharted.

There are vague references in Homer to one Zakynthos who set off from Arcadia in the Peloponnese accompanied by his men to colonise the island. As time went by the settlers increased in number; they grew prosperous and spread to other islands, setting up colonies on Paros and Crete and even further afield on the Iberian Peninsula.

Thucydides, however, refers to the first settlers on Zakynthos as being from Achaia.

From Homer's "Iliad", we can conclude that Zakynthos, together with the other Ionian islands

of Kephallonia and Lefkada, which often shared the same fate as Zakynthos, and Acarnania in Central Greece, were part of the domain of Odysseus, the legendary king of Ithaca, who took twelve ships to the siege of Troy and was subsequently to undergo a great many trials and adventures. Homer calls Odysseus's men "Kephallines" and tells us that they were brave warriors. Later with the help of Neoptolemus they managed to overthrow Odysseus's domination and gain their independence.

The worship of Apollo, Artemis, Dionysus, Aphrodite and other Olympian deities was widespread on Zakynthos, as we can see from various myths and ancient coins which have been found in the area. It is clear that the settlers from the mainland brought with them elements from their religion and their culture.

Nowhere is there any mention of participation of Zakynthos in the Persian Wars, and it is quite likely that the island maintained a neutral position.

In the prolonged conflict between the two most powerful Greek cities, Athens and Sparta, for domination of mainland Greece, Zakynthos took the side of the Spartans. When

Left:
The 17th century church of Aghios Nikolaos tou Molou on Solomos square.

Below:
Aghia Mavra, at Machairado.

in 456 B.C. the Athenian fleet triumphed over the Spartans, the Zakynthians along with other former allies of the defeated side joined the Athenian League.

During the Peloponnesian War the Zakynthians took the side of the Corfiotes against the Corinthians in a triumphant naval battle near Lefkimmi on Corfu in 434 B.C. Four years later the Lacedaemonians decided to regain their influence on Zakynthos, but despite the powerful forces at their disposal they were unsuccessful. In the end Zakynthos took part alongside the Athenians in the ill-fated Sicilian expedition, the disastrous result of which was the dissolution of the League and the reannexation of Zakynthos by the Lacedaemonians.

The island later came under the domination of the newly emerging power of Macedonia (217 B.C.), as her location and her wealth became a target of the expansionist tendencies of the Macedonians. Zakynthos was subsequently occupied by the Romans, who sold the island to the Achaians in 191 B.C. but not long after recaptured it thanks to the rhetorical skill of the Roman general Titus Flaminius, who persuaded the Achaians that Zakynthos rightfully belonged to the Romans since it had been given to them as a reward for bravery.

During the era of Roman occupation the island was initially governed by a Roman proconsul, in accordance with Roman law, but it later gained its independence and was governed by its own laws, although it was obliged to supply men for the Roman army and pay taxes to the Roman treasury. During the first few years after Roman law was enforced, the people of Zakynthos revolted several times against occupation by a foreign power, and as a result frequently came up against the Roman garrison on the island. On other occasions, the local residents helped the Romans to defend the island, as happened in 87 B.C. when together they put up a stout resistance to the siege by General Archelaus, who had been sent

Zakynthian
stater
(5th cent. B.C.)

Roman coin
of Zakynthos
(2d cent, A.D.)

by Mithridates to place the island in bondage.
The people of Zakynthos also joined forces
with the Roman army to fend off pirates who
roamed the seas raiding the Ionian islands and
the coasts of the Western Mediterranean during the pre-Christian period. Initially the pirates succeeded in gaining the upper hand,

but later the Roman commander Pompey retook the island with his well-drilled fleet, augmented by local men. This did not, however, solve the problem of pirate raids which, as we shall see, were to continue to plague the islanders through the Byzantine era, too.

When the Roman territories were split into provinces, Zakynthos, together with the other islands (except Crete), became part of the province of Achaia. Later it was included in the province of Illyria and eventually formed the separate Theme of Kephallonia, along with the other Ionian islands.

The dawn of the Byzantine era saw Zakynthos weighed down by adversity. During the years when the Roman Empire was on the decline and was facing problems of survival and internal stability, the remoter areas, such as Zakynthos, had already been abandoned to their fate and were at the mercy of all kinds of invaders: Goths, Vandals, Arabs, Saracens, etc.

Invasion and looting of the island continued throughout the Byzantine era, with relatively long intervals between attacks when Zakynthos managed to achieve some degree of reconstruction. However, these repeated barbaric blows prevented the people of Zakynthos from getting on with any creative work, since their one concern was to be on the alert to protect their island.

It was during these difficult times that Christianity came to Zakynthos, a new religion that proclaimed love and peace between nations; these were visions that held a strong attraction for the beleaguered Zakynthians, who were quickly converted. According to local folklore, it was on Zakynthos that Mary Magdalene first preached the Word of God; the village where she taught was called Mariès, and a celebration in her memory is carried out there every year.

Simultaneously with the fall of Byzantium the Crusaders appeared on the scene from the West; on the pretext of liberating the Holy Lands, they raided the remotest provinces of

The unusual beltry of the church of St. Nicholas in the village of the same name.

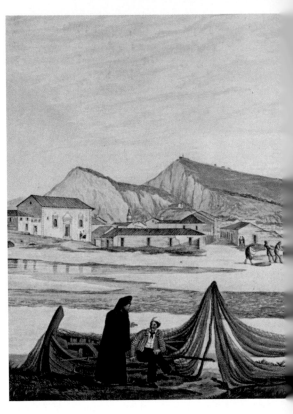

the Byzantine Empire which no longer had the power to come to their aid.

Returning from their campaigns in the Holy Lands, the Frankish noblemen and their troops, who usually consisted of every conceivable kind of adventurer, would endeavour to conquer the wealthy Byzantine provinces. Their designs would naturally include the nearby islands in the Ionian Sea. After a number of pillaging raids they captured Zakynthos and Kephallonia (1185), which from then on ceased to belong to the Byzantine Empire and constituted the County Palatine of Kephallonia and Zakynthos.

The various dynasties of Frankish noblemen governed the islands in a despotic fashion, denying the Greek population any freedom

Rare engraving of Zakynthos, the town and the harbour, by J. Cartwright, (1863).

and endeavouring to impose on them the Western Christian dogma. The dark age of Frankish rule on Zakynthos was characterised by murder, intrigue, conspiracy and every form of violence. With such a situation on the domestic front the County was unable to deal with dangers from foreign foes, and in a clash with the Turkish fleet the Franks were overcome and forced to agree to the payment of an annual tax before a peace treaty with the Turks could be signed. However, the Turks then began to look for an opportunity to take control of the island; this opportunity presented itself when the Franks were late in paying their tax one year and the Turks went on the rampage, pillaging and looting the island. They threw out the Franks and installed their own garrison (1479).

Turkish occupation of Zakynthos, however, was to last only five years. During this period, the Venetians were a major naval and trading power. They were the rulers of the Mediterranean, and their ambitious plans included domination of the Ionian islands. Their chance came in 1484 when they drew up a treaty with the Turks, under the terms of which they would govern the island in return for paying the Sultan an annual sum of 500 gold ducats.

Thus began the age of Venetian rule for Zakynthos, which was to last until 1797. During these three centuries the island saw greater prosperity than it had ever known in its hitherto stormy history.

It was an age when new ideas, a new culture and new social models were brought to the island on a large scale and with very little control exercised over the manner in which they were introduced. Great leaps forward were taken in a very short space of time, and the people of Zakynthos were obliged to keep pace; they had no choice - they were simply swept along by the tide. Clearly a new era was being born which was to have an immediate effect on the social, intellectual and economic life of the island.

The fact that the authorities provided incentives to encourage as many Venetians as possible to come and settle on Zakynthos meant that there was a sharp increase in the island's population, and this was understandably accompanied by a pronounced western influence on the manners, customs and occupations of the local residents, and even on the language, with the introduction of many Italian words. The Zakynthians manifested a discreet receptivity and self-restraint in the face of this flood of foreign influences. There is no doubt that they took a great deal from the newcomers to their island, but they never turned their backs on what was truly theirs. They assimilated each new element into their culture and infused it with their own island spirit, miraculously blending and balancing

Buondelmonti: Water colour of Zakynthos, 16th cent. (Gennadios Library, Athens).

the two components. At the same time they instilled into their foreign occupiers many elements of Zakynthian culture. This interaction, which is discernible across the whole spectrum of artistic creation during the period of Venetian rule and part of the period that followed, proved to be extremely successful. However, the most significant characteristic of the years to which we refer was the feeling of calm and security which prevailed on the island and which laid the foundations for reconstruction and creativity in a place which had been devastated by successive invasions.

With the coming of the Italians the population, as we have said, increased considerably, and the confined space of the mediaeval settlement in the Kastro into which the local people squeezed to hide from marauding pirates no longer sufficed. The newcomers therefore began to build their houses outside the limits of the old settlement, and eventually spread right down to the harbour. As the Italians had a long tradition in town planning they attached considerable importance to the harmonious development of the town and to the layout of its streets. They also embellished the

17th century engraving. Map of Zakynthos (D. Zivas collection).

Zakynthian capital with open squares, based on Italian models, and many grand houses.

The social, political and economic life of the island was revitalised. The government was an aristocratic one, the top-ranking nobleman being the Provveditore (governor) who was invested with administrative, military and judicial powers. Side by side with him was the Council of Noblemen, which was responsible for electing the Provveditore.

Three social classes developed on the Venetian-occupied island: the nobility, the bourgeoisie and the populace (from the Italian "il popolo", meaning "the people"). To the first of these belonged the landowners who were registered in the Golden Book, the book of the nobility. The second class comprised merchants and tradesmen, and the third consisted of farmers, labourers and sailors. Only the nobility had any civil rights. The position of working class people was deplorable, as they were harshly treated by the aristocracy who exploited them by using them as slaves on their estates. Unable to tolerate the oppression and injustice any longer, the "populari" rose up against the ruling class, boldly demanding humane living conditions. This social explosion, known as the People's Rebellion, ended in a blood bath (1628-1632). It was the first uprising in the history of modern Greece and is therefore an important landmark in any study of events on the island of Zakynthos.

As time went by, the Venetian domination of the Mediterranean began to be eroded; the reasons for this are to be found in the system of misgovernment, the oppression of the lower classes who from time to time staged uprisings and instigated social unrest, the frequent clashes with the Turks and the spreading of the doctrine of the French Revolution, which called upon the working classes to unite against any form of tyranny and fight for their freedom. The message was eagerly received on Zakynthos where the populace was suffering from the harsh treatment by the nobility, and the seeds of revolution, once sown, quickly flourished. Taking inspiration from the French Revolution, the patriotic people of Zakynthos formed a political organisation called the Jacobin Association, whose object was to grant all citizens equal rights and put an end to the undisguised exploitation of the populace by the nobility. It was during this insurrection

that Venetian rule finally crumbled. On July, 4th 1797, amid demonstrations of enthusiasm and relief, the island was handed over by the Venetians to the French Republicans.

There followed the spectacular burning of the Golden Book of the nobility and of their family shields in the town's central square to symbolise the abolition of social inequality. The populace now demanded the institution of a democratic government in which the nobility had no part, and the abolition of courtesy titles.

Zakynthos was designated as the capital of the Prefecture of the Ionian; the island established its own local administration and set about the task of rehabilitation, despite the machinations of the nobility, who did their utmost to regain the privileges they had lost by placing obstacles in its path.

Three years later, in March 1800, Russia and Turkey signed a treaty whereby the Ionian Islands became an autonomous state known as the Septinsular Republic; this form of government was not really so strange given that the Republic belonged administratively to the Russian Empire but at the same time paid an annual tax to the Turks.

During the period which followed, until the coming of British rule in 1809, a series of events took place involving the nobility and the Great Powers, of which the predominant concern was the promotion of their own interests. Once again the ordinary people were trampled under foot and obliged to watch their fate being decided by those in power.

On September, 19th 1809, the British assumed control of the island and set up the Ionian State with Zakynthos as its capital.

The first few years of British rule were creative ones in which the local people and their captors worked together to restore all aspects of the island's life. In 1814, however, with the consent of the other major powers, Britain took over the "protection" of the United States of the

*Monument
to the members
of the Philiki
Etairia.*

Ionian Isles, as they were now called, and Zakynthos along with the other Ionian Islands became a British protectorate. All power was now
concentrated in the hands of the British governor who ruled the island in accordance with
the terms of an autocratic constitution.

This, by and large, was the situation in which
the Ionian Islands found themselves at the
outbreak of the Greek Revolution in 1821.
During the years which preceded the uprising, the people of Zakynthos made an active
contribution to its organisation by taking a
number of important initiatives. Many were
chosen to become members of the so-called
"Philiki Etairia", or "Friendly Society", and
took the oath in the church of Agios Georgios
which is situated on a hill behind the town; it
is for this reason that the church is known as
"Agios Georgios ton Philikon".

Many a Zakynthian took part in battles fought
against the Turks in the Peloponnese. There
was also a Committee for the National Struggle
on the island, which had much to offer during
these critical times for the Greek nation.

The people of Zakynthos and the other Ionian Islands, who did not live under the Turkish yoke, had a good deal more freedom of movement than the enslaved Greeks, who were trying to organise themselves amid great secrecy under the watchful eye of their captor.

In order to avoid friction with the Ottoman Empire, and also because they too were in the position of conquerors, the British naturally sided with the Turks and viewed any kind of movement towards liberation with mistrust, putting every possible obstacle in the way of attempts by the people under their dominion to come to the aid of struggling Greece.

Nevertheless, despite the opposition of the British, the islanders succeeded in amassing a considerable sum of money to give financial support to the national struggle, and to provide food and munitions for the besieged people of Missolonghi by breaking through the cordon round the town with their ships. Many refugees from the heroic Exodus from Missolonghi, mainly women and children, were given food and shelter on the island of Zakynthos.

The revolt of the enslaved Greek nation gave heart to the people of the Ionian Islands and was the spark which set off their own struggle for liberation. They learned from the sacrifices made by the Greeks and realised that their own fetters were no less oppressive. Harsh government, social inequality and exploitation by both foreign powers and the rich who enjoyed foreign favour had finally become intolerable.

They opted to join the struggle and through it succeeded in achieving a number of modifications to the autocratic constitution laid down by the British.

Their greatest accomplishment lay in gaining the consent of their "protectors" to set up political parties, thereby reestablishing political activity on the island and giving the people the right to speak and make demands through their representatives.

In the first free elections in February 1850,

Above: Monastery of Aghios Georgios.

Below: Aghios Haralambos, at Machairado.

forty Zakynthos citizens were elected to represent the people in the Ionian Parliament. The struggle for liberation was thus transferred to the parliamentary chamber. Thirteen years later the British were forced by the situation that had been created to agree to a treaty uniting the Ionian Islands with free Greece (1863). Thus after six centuries of occupation, Zakynthos joined her fate with that of Greece so that they could march together along the difficult road towards reconstruction and progress.

In subsequent history the island was to be subjected, along with the rest of the country, to occupation by the Italians and the Germans. Hundreds of citizens organised themselves into a resistance movement against the occupying army and after much conflict and sacrifice the island was liberated.

However, this was not to be the end of Zakynthos's misfortunes. A few years after the liberation, Fate had a terrible ordeal in store for the island, which human endeavour was quite inadequate to cope with. One summer's day in August, 1953, a violent earthquake shook the island. The strong earth tremors razed the beautiful town with its tall mansion-houses to the ground; the elegant arcades were reduced to rubble, the majestic buildings flattened and the picturesque little alleyways completely destroyed. The whole island was turned into a miserable heap of ruins.

Once they had recovered from this unexpected blow, the people of Zakynthos mustered their strength and with government help set about the task of rebuilding their island. These were difficult times, but armed with perseverance and optimism they set to work and painstakingly rebuilt a new Zakynthos on the model of the old one, endeavouring to retain the character, charm and unique quality of their town, an effort in which they were partially successful.

Pictures of Zakynthos following the destructive earthquake.

The distinct lack of archaeological treasures on the island can probably be accounted for by the tremendous geological realignments that took place in the Ionian region. A few items of archaeological interest - mainly coins - have survived and here and there some ancient ruined temples have been discovered. Parts of an ancient acropolis have also been found near the citadel. A number of churches containing wall paintings and some icons of limited interest have survived from the Byzantine era.

Zakynthos leapt up from obscurity and began to achieve great things in the arts and letters during the course of the 15th century when the island was under Venetian rule. We see the curious but not inexplicable phenomenon that, while mainland Greece languished and suffered the humiliations of the Turkish yoke, the Ionian Islands experienced a rapid blossoming of culture the like of which they had never seen before in all their long history and which spread swiftly to all the arts.

There was an unprecedented and frenzied surge of activity in every field of artistic creation, whether the means of expression involved the use of words, the paintbrush, the chisel or musical notation.

Under Venetian rule the islands were to experience a sophisticated and culturally developed occupying power which introduced them to the special idioms of western culture, in contrast to mainland Greece which was deprived not only of its freedom as a nation but even of freedom of thought and expression - fundamental preconditions for any cultural creativity.

The people of Zakynthos, along with the other Ionian islanders, were not unreceptive to these western influences. It is obvious in all the art forms that during this period local artists and scholars grasped the elements imported from

The statue of Dionysios Solomos.

abroad and imbued them with their own distinctive characteristics based on local tradition and heritage; their work is therefore never a mere imitation of foreign models but original creations in their own right, many of them outstanding examples of their particular genre.

Moreover - and this is something that has occurred many times in the history of Greece - there is always a degree of ambiguity with regard to influences in the artistic and intellectual spheres, that is to say, they frequently work in two directions: from the captor to the captive and vice versa; and this is confirmation that the island had a strong and healthy tradition of its own.

PAINTING

Iconographers who originally hailed from several different parts of Greece lived on the island of Zakynthos. The most important of these were Michail Damaskinos (who painted the icons in the Church of Ag. Dimitrios tou Kolla), Dimitrios and Georgios Moschos (who were responsible for painting the holy pictures in the Church of Ag. Ioannis ton Logotheton), Manolis and Constantinos Tzannes, and Stephanos Tzangarolas, who painted the "Adoration of the Shepherds" (now in the National Gallery in Athens). The Italian influence is clearly evident in this work, although it was painted using the Byzantine technique.

By the 17th century, the plastic arts had become highly developed in the Ionian Islands, with painting leading the field. There was a clear western influence which manifested itself not only in the choice of subjects but also in changes in technique; Panayiotis Doxaras now used oils on canvas instead of egg tempera on wood. This meant a tremendous revolution in style and opened up greater possibilities for portrait painting and perspective drawing.

Panayiotis Doxaras was the pioneer of this new style that revolutionised the painting of the age,

The *"Adoration of the Shepherds"* by *Stephanos Tzangarolas.* *(National Gallery Athens).*

and he is therefore considered as one of the founders of the Ionian School. There are pictures painted by him in the Church of Our Lady of the Angels (Kyria ton Angelon) in Zakynthos. The National Gallery in Athens houses some of his portraits which reveal both the innovative Italian approach and the artist's endeavour not to stray too far from the traditional mode of expression and the austerity of Byzantine Art. The result, particularly in his religious works, is a mixture of the Byzantine and the Italian styles.

It was the Ionian painters, most of whom had studied in Italy, who brought western art to

59

Dionysios Tsokos, «Portrait of a Lady» (National Gallery, Athens).

Greece. Apart from Panayiotis Doxaras, the most famous of them were his son, Nikolaos Doxaras, who painted the icons in the Church of the Panagia tis Faneromenis in Zakynthos, and Nikolaos Koutouzis (1741-1813), whose work "Lady with the White Gloves" is in the National Gallery in Athens and is arguably the best portrait of the period. These two painters devoted themselves almost entirely to religious themes and did not endow their work with any nationalist overtones.

However, the self-taught painter Nikolaos Koundounis (1768-1834) was later to produce religious works which had a strong nationalist element. When he was accused of being a member of the Philiki Etairia and exiled from Kephallonia to the uninhabited island of Dia, he painted four pictures which together as a group quite clearly convey nationalist messages. During the period in which he lived and was active as a member of the Etairia, considerable

Nikolaos Koutouzis, «Portrait of a Lady wearing a diadem».

progress had been made in the evolution of a national conscience and the idea of uniting Zakynthos with mainland Greece had already taken hold.

Koundounis also painted several portraits, some of which ("Self-portrait", "Old Woman with Cup" and "Noblewoman with Coat of Arms") hang in the National Gallery. His self-portrait is deemed to be a milestone in the evolution of the Ionian School. Although he was influenced by Koutouzis and other of his contemporaries who taught him how to use colour, some elements from the Byzantine tradition of which the artist himself was possibly unaware are discernible in his work.

Dionysios Tsokos (1820-1862) gave psychological overtones to his portraits. His "Lady Arrayed in the Dress of Queen Amalia" and a painting of Dionatos Demoulitsas (National Gallery) are examples of such portraits in which the artist manages to convey with great sensitivity the internal suffering of the sick woman and Demoulitsas's determination and zest for life. An example of his highly developed technique lies in his minimal use of colour. Portraits of the 1821 freedom-fighters which were commissioned by the Greek government are now housed in the Athens Museum of History and Folk Art. These, too, reveal not only the painter's skill in conveying the face's internal expression but also his masterful eye for detail and the clarity with which he portrays all the external features (dress, jewellery, hairstyles, etc.).

Tsokos's work was so highly thought of that in 1847, when he was still quite a young man, he was made a member of the Panel of Judges at the Polytechnic School.

An important Zakynthian painter of the 19th century who won international acclaim for his versatility was Dimitris Pelekasis. His icons, landscapes and portraits earned him many distinctions, and there are works by him in churches, museums and private collections on Zakynthos. He also earned a name for himself as preserver of paintings and organiser of museums and collections, and it was he who set up the Zakynthos Museum.

During the 17th and at the beginning of the 18th century the Ionian School confined itself to the painting of icons and religious themes. However, from the end of the 18th century after the Liberation and throughout most of the 19th century there were great changes in secular painting. The subjects now cultivated were the historic scenes that were immensely popular in Western Europe at the time. A prolific number of such paintings was produced and their success depended upon the ability of the artist to convey depth and perspective. A subdivision of this category is portrait-painting, which provides us with pictures of the more important people of the period: kings, generals, freedom-fighters and other notable personalities of the age.

In addition to the popular genre scenes, sea and landscapes, this period also saw the shy emergence of still life and nude paintings which were enjoying tremendous popularity in Western Europe.

An important contribution made by the Ionian artists was that they brought secular painting to the Ionian Islands from the West, and in so doing they opened the doors to a broader, more modern form of artistic expression. As a result of the movement that began in the Ionian Islands, people began to hang pictures in their houses and see them not merely as a way of depicting holy figures and scenes in the church, but also as works of art which could be enjoyed in other places as well.

SCULPTURE

Silver engraving and wood carving flourished on Zakynthos during the 18th century. Both appeared mainly in the churches. A famous silver engraver was Georgios Bafas, and examples of his work (a large icon of St. Dionysios, a reliquary, and a vessel in which the saint's hand is

Aghios Dionysios. The impressive carved iconostasis.

kept) are to be found in the church of Ag. Dionysios.

Two important wood carvers whose work adorned many churches and mansions were the brothers Andravidiotis and Anastasios Vlachos. However, most of their work was destroyed in the earthquakes that hit the island in 1953.

LITERATURE

Literature began to flourish on the island during the 15th century. Zakynthian writers were distinguished not only for their poetry and prose, but also for their translations of works in classical Greek into the language of the period. The island's literary efforts were greatly helped by the fact that a considerable number of works were printed in Venice, an important centre for arts and literature at that time.

The interest and response shown by the public, both at home and abroad, were immense and naturally provided a valuable incentive for literary creation.

Monument to Foscolo.

One of the most illustrious men of letters on

*Bust of
the poet
Ugo Foscolo.*

15th century Zakynthos was Nikolaos Loukanis, a poet and very able translator of Homer's "Iliad" which was reprinted three times, the original edition being published in Venice.

Other writers included Pachomios Roussanos, who was the author of codices in Greek, Dimitrios Zenos, who translated the "Batrachomyomachia", Tzannes Koronaios, who wrote a major piece of rhyming poetry entitled "The Exploits of Mercurius Bois", and Angelos Soumakis, author of "An Account of the People's Rebellion". The Zakynthian scholar and philosopher of the 18th century, Evgenios Voulgaris, was an ardent supporter of archaicism, one of his major works being "Logic". Contemporaries of his included Andreas Sigouros and the priest Antonios Martelaos, who was the teacher of Dionysios Solomos, the Italo-Zakynthian Ugo Foscolo and Gouzelis.

Dimitris Gouzelis wrote a comedy in verse entitled "Chasis" productions of which are performed in the theatre even today.

Antonios Matesis's tragedy "The Monarchist" is considered to be the foundation stone of modern Greek theatre.

Georgios Tertsetis (1800-1874), a member of the judiciary who was a friend and student of Solomos, took part in the trial of the Old Man of Morias (the nickname of Theodoros Kolokotronis) and opposed his conviction. He was a man of many talents, writing both poetry and prose works which included "The Memoirs of Kolokotronis".

The island of Zakynthos had the privilege of being the birthplace of the two greatest Greek poets of the 19th century.

Andreas Kalvos (1792-1869), one of the leading modern Greek poets, was born in Zakynthos but spent most of his life in various European countries - Italy, Switzerland, France and Britain. In Italy he became a friend of Foscolo who helped him with his work; and it was while he was in Italy that he was initiated into the Italian liberation movement and became a member of the Carbonari. He worked in Europe as a private tutor, returning to Greece in 1821 with the outbreak of the War of Independence to offer his services to the struggle. He encountered a great deal of discord, however, and disappointed and bitter took himself off to the island of Corfu, where he lived for 24 years, earning a living by teaching. He finally settled in Britain where he stayed until his death in 1869.

His work is varied but not extensive. He wrote a number of verse tragedies in Italian, including "Theramenes" and "Danaides"; in Greek he wrote his "Odes", twenty seminal poems full of musicality which were inspired by the 1821 Revolution. The language he used was for the most part the idiosyncratic, pseudo-classical language known as "purist" (katharevousa) but it also contained a number of elements from popular

Greek. Kalvos developed a verse form entirely his own, and his regular stanzas are echoes of Pindar, the Byzantine hymnographers and demotic songs. Kalvos's peculiar kind of blank verse gives us an independent style of poetry that is wholly Greek and exudes archaic splendour. The line "Freedom demands virtue and daring" is an eternal message, an everlasting trumpet-call to all freedom-loving nations everywhere to join the struggle.

Dionysios Solomos, Greece's National Poet, was born in Zakynthos in 1798 and died in Corfu in 1857. The first verses of his "Hymn to Liberty", which were set to music by the Corfiote composer N. Mantzaros-Chalkiopoulos were designated as the Greek National Anthem in 1864. As a

Dionysios
Solomos.

Above:
Mausoleum
of Solomos
and Kalvos.

Below:
Room in the
Solomos
Museum.

young man he went to Italy where he studied law, literature and philosophy in Venice, Cremona and Pavia. The period he spent studying Italian literature was to have a major influence on the formation of his character and his work. While in Italy he wrote a number of poems in Italian. On returning to Zakynthos he embarked upon a serious study of the demotic songs which he so much admired, and under the guidance of his friend Spiridon Trikoupis began to write poems in Greek. Trikoupis persuaded him that Italy did not need his creative genius whereas the Greek people, who were at that time revolting against the Turkish yoke, had a great need for a poet who would interpret their hopes and expectations and their passions in his poetry and boost their spirits during this difficult struggle. Thus in 1823, at the age of 25, he wrote his "Hymn to Liberty" within the space of a month. It is an inspired work which gave encouragement to the warring nation.

In his mature years Dionysios Solomos wrote "The Free Besieged" which represented the pinnacle of his poetic genius. Its fifteen-syllable lines are written in a somewhat fragmented style. By nature a perfectionist, Solomos was unwilling to finish his poems with lines that were of inferior quality, and this is the reason why all his major works are of a fragmented nature.

Amongst his most important works are "Epigram of the Fishermen", "Poisoned Woman", "To a Nun", "Lambros", "Kritikos", "Porphyras" and "Nikiphoros Vryennios".

Solomos also wrote prose pieces; the most famous of these are his "Dialogue", in which he expresses in dialogue form his personal views on the language question, and "Woman of Zakynthos" in which he lashes out against the indifference shown in certain Greek circles towards the tragedy of the people of Missolonghi in the wake of the Exodus from the town.

The reputation of Dionysios Solomos is international; his influence on the evolution of modern Greek poetry and the victory of demotic or popular Greek over the katharevousa is of immense importance. His work represents the apex in lyric composition in modern Greek literature.

In 1865 Solomos's remains were transferred from Corfu to Zakynthos and buried in a splendid tomb beside that of Andreas Kalvos. A statue was erected in his honour in the Plateia

Eleftherias (Freedom Square) otherwise known as Solomos Square, in Zakynthos town.

After his death an entire school of poets called the Ionian School grew up, based on the style and ideas of Solomos. Its chief luminaries were Iakovos Polylas and Ioulios Typaldos, and it included in its ranks such great men of Zakynthos as Georgios Tertsetis and Andreas and Stephanos Martzokis.

Another famous modern Greek writer, Grigorios Xenopoulos (1867-1951), lived for many years on Zakynthos, although he was born in Constantinople and died in Athens. As well as being a writer of prose and theatrical works he was also a critic and journalist, and in 1931 became a member of the Academy. In 1927 he founded the literary journal "Nea Estia". He was a prolific writer, deriving inspiration for the majority of his prose works from life and society on his beloved Zakynthos which he looked upon as his homeland.

Xenopoulos made a tremendous contribution to children's literature as both a writer and a translator. It was he who first translated Jules Verne into Greek, enabling whole generations of Greek children to be brought up on Verne's imaginative and adventure-packed stories.

His theatrical opus is extensive. Many of his plays, such as "Temptation", "Il Fiore di Levante» ("The Flower of the Levant"), "Stella Violanti" and "The Countess Valerena's Secret" are still performed and continue to attract the public's interest.

He also made an invaluable contribution to the establishment of demotic or popular Greek in bourgeois fiction.

During the years of Venetian rule on the island, there was a great deal of creative activity in the sphere of popular or folk plays, influenced naturally by the Italian theatre. One type of amateur play written by unknown playwrights who were blessed with a natural talent were the so-called "Homilies"; these were performed out of doors, generally at carnival time. Improvisation, imper-

sonation, sketches lampooning various aspects of Zakynthian society, exaggerations of the truth, the grotesque presentation of social phenomena - all elements which indubitably sprang directly from the Italian Commedia dell'Arte and were adapted to the Ionian idiom - were the main features of this immensely enjoyable form of theatre so adored by the people of Zakynthos. Indeed, it is still very much alive today as a way to relax and escape from the routine of everyday life.

The "Homilies" were not, however, the only kind of theatre for which the people of Zakynthos had a passion: later they began to put on performances of ancient dramas, Cretan plays and works by contemporary Zakynthian playwrights (for example, Foscolo, Matesis, Gouzelis) in the theatres of Zakynthos.

The bust of Greece's national poet, Dionysios Solomos, on Strani hill.

MUSIC

As well as being theatre-lovers, the people of Zakynthos are also music-lovers. The island has a long and rich musical tradition which developed during the years of Venetian rule, and as a result

71

was inevitably subjected to the influence of western music. As an art form, music went hand in hand with the theatre and every other kind of artistic display, folk festivals, processions and military parades. Musical education was consolidated with the establishment in 1815 of the Zakynthos School of Music by the Italian music professor Marco Battaglia, and a short while later the setting-up of the municipal orchestra.

Notable 19th century Zakynthian musicians include Frangiscos Domeneghinis, Antonios Kapnissis and Pavlos Carrer, while Georgios Planyteros, Dionysios Latas and Panayiotis Gritzanis are outstanding examples of the Ionian ecclesiastical musical tradition.

The Zakynthian composer, Georgios Kostis, is famed for his melodious "Cantades" that were and still are sung today on the island with such feeling. The Cantada, which made its first appearance in the Ionian Islands and flourished particularly on Kephallonia, is quite different from the local folk songs of the rest of Greece, both on the mainland and in the islands. It is a polyphonic choral piece of Italian origin, with guitar or mandolin accompaniment. The verses, some of which are written by lyric-writers while others are performed ex tempore, deal with the theme of love.

In closing this chapter on the intellectual and artistic achievements of the peaceful Ionian island of Zakynthos, we cannot fail to be struck by the extraordinary volume and quality of these achievements, considering the size of the place. If we were to attempt to interpret this phenomenon, we should probably conclude that it is the result of favourable historical circumstances and the complex nature of the Zakynthian people, whose devotion to all that is beautiful - the "κάλλος" of the ancient Greeks - in all its forms of expression, knows no bounds.

"Il Fiore di Levante" ("The Flower of the Levant"), which was the complimentary title the Venetians gave to the island, held sway over an

area that was not easily conquered, that of Civil-
isation, at a time when the permanent claimants
to control over it were the countries of the re-
fined and "civilised" West. Zakynthos thus e-
merged the winner in two contests: it dominated as an intellectual and artistic entity, and at
the same time served as a harmonious link between the cultures of the East and West, pro-
ducing highly original works against a broader
spectrum of artistic creation.

ARCHITECTURE

The special links between Zakynthos and the
West and the various historical, political and social conditions prevailing in Greece from the
11th to the 19th centuries are amongst a number of factors that contributed to the creation of
a quite distinct architectural style. From the end
of the 17th century onwards the tremendous
upturn in the Arts and Letters went hand in
hand with staggering developments in the field

*A sample of
Zakynthian
architecture.*

of architecture. There was an obvious proclivity towards Western models which bore marked traces of the Renaissance, Baroque and Mannerist styles but at the same time retained a local Ionian character.

Around the end of the 18th century the main towns of the Ionian Islands Corfu, Argostoli and Zakynthos, had assumed a definite form which included magnificent mansion-houses, neat middle- and working-class homes and numerous churches, all of them revealing the extent to which Ionian achitecture had developed.

The Venetians for their part attended to various constructions that were of a defensive nature or of public benefit, such as roads, public buildings, bridges, a sewage network, etc. To judge from these well-designed projects and from the information available, there were in the Ionian Islands many excellent craftsmen who organised themselves into guilds according to their skill.

Later as Neoclassicism swept through Europe this new style began to be popular in the Ionian

Right: Characteristic arcades on a street in Zakynthos.

Below: A room in the Komoutos mansion.

St. Mark's square.
Lithograph from J. Cartwright's "Views in the Ionian Islands".

Islands, leaving its stamp on official buildings and working-class houses alike. Between 1840 and 1870 several Neoclassical buildings were erected in Zakynthos which showed signs of both local and Venetian influence as well as some traces of the Baroque style. A typical building of this period was the Zakynthos Club on the central square of Agios Markos. Unfortunately the building now exists only on paper in the form of plans and old photographs; it was completely destroyed by the devastating earthquakes of 1953.

The year 1875 saw the completion of the imposing Municipal Theatre building in Zakynthos town which was designed by the well-known German architect of the period, E. Ziller; this building, which was on Solomos Square, also housed the Lombard Club. It sustained a certain amount of damage in the earthquake of 1893 and was eventually completely destroyed in 1953. The Theatre was one of the most memorable buildings which belonged to the late Neoclassical period at the end of the 19th century.

The Neoclassical style also influenced church design. A typical example of a Neoclassical church is that of Ag. Marina, in the village of the same name (formerly known as Fagia).

There were once many outstanding Neoclassical houses, both mansions and working-class homes, in Zakynthos town itself and in the villages; very few of them still remain. The most characteristic is the country home of the Lunzi family, known as the "Sarakina", which is located a little way inland from Laganas near the village of Pantokratoras. It is one of the few buildings to remain standing after the earthquakes. Sadly most of the structures which adorned the town of Zakynthos and the picturesque "folk-style" homes of the working people in the villages no longer exist.

However, Zakynthos emerged from the ruins reborn and renewed, with many fine new buildings such as the Government House in Alexandros Romas Street, the Law Courts in Tertsetis Street, and the splendid edifices that flank Solomos Square. The town's squares were rebuilt and the famous Strada Marina along the seafront restored.

There is a series of photographs of old Zakynthos in the Municipal Cultural Centre which the visitor would do well to peruse in order to gain an idea of the town's former glory. The Zakynthos of these touching old photographs is still very much alive in the hearts of the older residents who knew and loved the place well.

Pictures of old Zakynthos.

*Above:
One of the main
streets of the
town leading
into St. Mark's
square.*

*Right: Solomos
square and the
church of Aghios
Nikolaos tou
Molou.*

Full of life and movement, Zakynthos has an air of festivity and action; cruise-ships call in at the harbour and move on and luxury yachts lie at anchor offshore, while boats of every ilk come and go constantly, loading and discharging their cheerful throngs of passengers from all corners of the earth, who dash off from the harbour to one of the many popular beaches or a deserted cove to bask in the sun, frolic in the sea, enjoy an ouzo at some traditional ouzeri or a cup of coffee on a shady knoll with a view out over the azure waters of the Ionian Sea.

In the evening a visit to the disco, after first enjoying a delicious meal of fresh fish and international or (preferably) local cuisine at one of the many fish-houses, restaurants, grills or traditional little tavernas scattered around the island...

The night hours have their own particular magic, the lights, the music and the little par-

ties of friends strolling along the beach all contributing to the aura of gaiety and good humour. On the other hand, there are plenty of secluded spots for those who prefer a little peace and quiet and whose idea of relaxation is a walk beside the sea or through the forest, where the scent of the pines mingles with the salty tang of the sea - or maybe a romantic wander by moonlight down a little alleyway in Zakynthos town.

These are all scenes from summertime on Zakynthos, when the place fairly throbs with life and is inundated by the hordes of visitors who flock to the island.

In winter the aspect changes. There are fewer ships in the harbour, the pace of life slows down and there is generally an air of greater tranquillity. The few tourists who are still here enjoy the peace and quiet, and have a chance now to get to know the real Zakynthos and its people, away from the strains of imported music and the lights of the busy nightclubs. The tourist season lasts from Easter till the end of September, reaching a peak during the months of July and August.

Zakynthos Carnival in the middle of the winter, one of the most famous of Greek carnival celebrations, attracts a lot of visitors who come to enjoy the local traditions.

The island has many hotels which are quite able to meet visitors' demands with regard to both the facilities they offer and their tariffs.

There is also plenty of tourist accommodation both in the town itself and at the various summer resorts: small guesthouses, furnished apartments and rooms to rent, all well-appointed with the requisite amenities for a pleasant and inexpensive stay. Most of them are scattered along the beach areas and in the villages (e.g. Alykes, Argasi, Vassilikos, Laganas, Planos, etc.). For lovers of the outdoor life there are campsites that comply with international standards at the villages of Lithakia and Tragaki.

The "Blue Grotto".

Right, above: Argasi. Below: Kalamaki.

All types of consumer goods are available in the town's stores while folk art shops, jewellers and various boutiques offer a selection of souvenirs for the visitor to take home as a memento of his holiday. Typical local products include a confection made from roasted almonds, known as "mandolato", the island's cheese and a jasmine-scented perfume.

The island offers ample opportunities for water sports. In addition to swimming and underwater fishing in the sparkling clear waters, the visitor can turn his hand to sailing, windsurfing and water-skiing. Most of the main beaches operate a boat-hire service with schools for learning water sports.

There is a good local bus service on the island, with buses operating on a daily basis between Zakynthos town and most of the villages and beaches. It is also possible to take a taxi or rent a car or motorbike to tour the island. In addition, trips around the island by caïque to see the fascinating caves at Xyngia and the famous Blue Grotto are organised by a number of local travel agencies.

FOLK HERITAGE AND LOCAL FESTIVITIES

With the passing of the years the occupations and interests of the islanders changed. Progress came face to face with tradition, and like rivers in full spate, when modernisation and industrialisation were brought to the island they swept along with them old, well-loved habits and ways, human experiences and emotions... Yet amid the maelstrom of all

this development and change certain customs managed to survive and are still practised to-day with enthusiasm on the part of the young-er generation and nostalgia by the older gen-eration.

Religious festivals have remained almost un-touched by the passage of time. The religious part of a celebration (church service, proces-

The seafront and the church of Aghios Dionysios.

sion, etc.) is usually followed by a folk festival at which local dances and songs are performed and there is a great deal of eating and drinking. The main festivals are as follows:

17th December, the Feast of Ag. Dionysios, protector and patron saint of Zakynthos. On this day, the anniversary of the saint's death, his relics are carried in procession around the streets of the town accompanied by the municipal orchestra.

Born in Zakynthos in 1547, Dionysios renounced the world at an early age and became a monk. He was ordained Archbishop of Aegina and Poros but soon abdicated his archepiscopal throne in order to return to Zakynthos and officiate at the Church of Agios Nikolaos tou Molou. He eventually withdrew to the Monastery at Anafonitria near Volimes where he remained until his death on 17th December, 1622.

While he was living as a monk at Volimes his brother's assassin came to him and asked for his help as he was being sought by the Venetians. Dionysios hid him in his cell and then helped him to escape. After the 1953 earth-

Above:
Anafonitria
Monastery
General view.

Left:
Zoödochos
Pigi.

The church of Faneromeni. quakes his cell at Anafonitria Monastery was restored. He was buried in the Strofades Islands but on 24th August, 1717 his remains were transferred to Zakynthos where they are kept in the church named after him, in a silver reliquary engraved by Georgios Bafas.

24th August is the second feast-day of the patron saint of Zakynthos, and is the anniversary of the transfer of his relics to Zakynthos from the Strofades. It is a magnificent affair: in the late afternoon there is a procession around the town, which is carried out with much pomp and circumstance, and in the evening fireworks are let off. This is followed by two days of feasting and celebration.

On Easter Friday the Feast of Zoödochos Pigis (Chryssopigis) is celebrated in Bochali, on the outskirts of Zakynthos town. The religious part of the festival includes the procession of the Byzantine icon of Panagia Chryssopigi, dating from 810 A.D., through the streets, and this is followed by celebrations that last late into the night, with lambs roasted on the spit, dancing and singing of local songs.

On the Feast of St. Thomas, the first Sunday after Easter, the Feast of Aï Lipios takes place at Kalyteros when people from every corner of the island gather at the village's tavernas to enjoy the traditional lamb on the spit and the delicious local speciality of vegetable fritters, dancing to the music of the "tambourloniaka-ra" (as the Zakynthians call their traditional folk instruments).

On the first Sunday in June the celebrated festival of Agia Mavra takes place in the village of Machairado.

17th July is the Feast of Agia Marina in the village of Fagia (also known as Agia Marina).

Machairado. The superb belfry of the church of Aghia Mavra.

15th August is the Feast of Panagia Pikridiotissa.

Other local feast-days include the day of the Holy Trinity, Agia Varvara, Ascension Day, the Theotokos of Katastara in the village of that name, Faneromeni in the village of Kalipado, and Agios Iosif tou Samakou in the village of Gaitani.

The way in which the Passion is relived in the island's churches and monasteries during Holy Week is very moving; all the islanders participate with a spirit of great devoutness.

Holy Week is celebrated with particular religious ceremonial in Zakynthos. At two o'clock on Good Friday afternoon the procession of the Crucifix moves through the streets of the town, accompanied by the municipal orchestra. This tradition is unique to Zakynthos. The procession winds up in Solomos Square where the bishop mounts the rostrum and taking the Crucifix in his hands, calls for God's blessing on the faithful.

At four o'clock the next morning Christ's Epitaphios is ceremonially borne out of the Cathedral; this is the only incidence of the Epitaphios being carried in procession through the town. The procession returns to the church at dawn for the first Resurrection service, which is announced with the joyful ringing of church bells.

The second Resurrection service is held at midnight on Easter Saturday, when the cry of "Christos Anesti" ("Christ is Risen!") goes up all over the town and an air of festivity is provided by the ringing of bells and the sounding of ships' sirens from the boats anchored in the harbour. The magical quality of this special night is enhanced by the multi-coloured display of fireworks that light up the sky. Festivities reach their climax on Easter Day itself, which is the most important festival in the Orthodox calendar and is celebrated the length and breadth of the island with much singing and dancing and roasting of lambs on the spit. The Service of Agape is held in the churches in the latter part of the afternoon, and this includes Easter readings from the Gospels in several other languages besides Greek to emphasise the universal relevance of the Resurrection and the brotherhood of nations through the Christian faith.

At 7 p.m. on Easter Sunday the Feast of Agios Lazaros is celebrated in the church that bears his name; the solemn procession is followed by festivities that include singing, dancing and roasting lambs on the spit, and later in the evening fireworks are let off.

Procession of the Crucifix in old Zakynthos.

Zakynthos Carnival, one of the most famous in Greece, has its roots in the celebrated Ve-

Men's costumes: Nobleman (left) and "popolaros" (right).

netian carnival tradition left over from the days of Venetian rule, when the town went on a spree for fifteen whole days and nights, dancing and generally living it up in the Zakynthos and Lombard Clubs, the Kavarkina and the town's squares.

Amongst the carnival celebrations a special place was reserved for the so-called "Homilies", open-air amateur theatrical performances, which attracted large crowds. The Zakynthos Carnival has been revived today with great splendour and a fair degree of authenticity, thanks to the efforts of the island's cultural associations and various local organisations and the spontaneity of the islanders themselves, who set aside their daily business for a while and help to organise the festivities, gaining real pleasure from doing so, as in the good old days. Many Greeks and other visitors come to the island during Carnival to experience at first hand the atmosphere of fun that pervades the place at this time.

Weddings are another cause for celebration, when the entire village community takes part and joins in the local dances.

The folk dances of Zakynthos are particularly interesting, the most popular one being the "giargitos" which has its roots in the traditional Cretan dance called the "geranos" and was brought to Zakynthos by Cretan refugees. Both these dances represent the triumphant dance by Theseus after he had slain the Minotaur. Other dances include the "Volimiatikos", which is danced in and around Volimes, the "gaïtani", the "galariotikos", the "tsakistos", and the "galiandra" and "manfrena", the lasts two being of Italian origin.

There were many types of traditional costume on Zakynthos, depending on the social class to which its wearer belonged. The gentlemen of the nobility and the bourgeoisie wore garments of expensive material, silk stockings and shoes with buckles, while the ladies wore hats with veils and gold jewellery. The "populari" and the villagers wore simple garments made of cheap cloth, and this served as yet another way to distinguish between the classes.

As far as the island's cuisine is concerned, special mention should be made of the local "stifado", a kind of stew cooked with tender local onions that impart a very special flavour to the dish, the local lamb, cheese, vegetable fritters and the island's own wines.

There is a great deal of cultural activity on the island, including frequent theatrical performances, concerts and recitals, lectures and exhibitions. Thus the island of the Doxaras brothers, Tsokos, Solomos, Kalvos and so many other famous men retains its links with the Arts and Letters, perpetuating its strong cultural tradition and continuing to be a place of inspiration for many contemporary artists and writers.

ZAKYNTHOS TOWN

Approaching the harbour by boat the visitor sees the town of Zakynthos spread out before him, nestling idly inside the bay on the south-east coast of the island opposite the Peloponnese. Before it lies the open sea, to the south the verdant slopes of Mount Skopos, and everything is overlaid with an air of ancient nobility, a gentility which even the earthquakes were unable to quash.

The "Flower of the Levant" still blooms, bestowing on the Ionian Sea its own special kind of beauty. It would be no exaggeration to say that with its magnificent buildings, well-designed squares, elegant arcades, fine wrought-iron balconies, churches with splendid bell-towers, neat open spaces and parks, picturesque little streets and broad avenues,

Above:
Solomos
square.

Left:
General view
of the town.

103

Solomos square. monuments and statues dedicated to its distinguished offspring, this is one if the most captivating towns in the Ionian Islands.

The busy harbour works night and day as ships come and go from the quays, endlessly disgorging people and cars until there is scarcely room to move.

The Strada Marina or Lombard Avenue which encircles the harbour and is lined with hotels, restaurants, patisseries and shops of every kind is one of the town's busiest streets. It is well worth taking an evening stroll along this thoroughfare from Solomos Square at one end to the Church of Ag. Dionysios at the other to enjoy the refreshing breeze blowing across the sea from the Peloponnese and the twinkling lights of the ships moored along the quays, the buildings that flank the road and the street lamps reflected in the calm waters of the harbour.

In the wide open space of Solomos Square stand a statue of the poet and a bust of Ugo Foscolo. The marble base of Solomos's statue is engraved with the words of the second verse of his "Hymn to Liberty":

"Απ' τα κόκκαλα βγαλμένη
Των Ελλήνων τα ιερά
Και σαν πρώτα ανδριωμένη
Χαίρε, ω χαίρε, Ελευθεριά".

("Hail, O Liberty, wrung from the sacred bones of the Greeks and once more ready for the fray...").

The square is flanked by magnificent buildings with arched windows, arcades and columns where the Town Hall, the National Bank of Greece, the Zakynthos Museum, the Municipal Library and other public administration offices are housed. On one side of the square is the old Church of Ag. Nikolaos tou Molou where St. Dionysios officiated for a period of time. The church was built in the 17th

A main street.

Above:
Aghios Nikolaos
tou Molou.

Below:
The Museum of
Zakynthos.

century in the Renaissance style, its only Byzantine feature being the bell-tower. Nearby is the post-Byzantine Museum containing some important works by Zakynthian hagiographers (among them Nikolaos Koutouzis and Nikolaos Koundounis).

Leaving the harbour behind and moving to-

Solomos square with the statue of Greece's national poet.

wards the interior of the town a few streets away from Solomos Square, the visitor comes to St. Mark's Square which is closely linked with the island's struggle for independence. On July, 30th 1797, fired by enthusiasm at the end of Venetian rule, the people of Zakynthos gathered in this little square and set light to the so-called Golden Book and the coats of arms of the nobility who enjoyed the favour of and were the instruments of the Venetians.

Here on St. Mark's Square are the Catholic church of Agios Markos and the splendid Museum of Solomos and other Eminent Zakynthians.

At the other end of the Strada Marina is the Church of Agios Dionysios where the saint's reliquary and icon are kept along with other valuable icons. The church's magnificent belltower looks out over the harbour.

The town has several remarkable churches, including The Church of Our Lady of the Angels, Faneromeni and Panagia Pikridiotissa, with works by Cretan and local hagiographers.

OUTSIDE THE TOWN

The famous "Blue Grotto" is very much worth a visit.

By taking one of the steep roads that lead out of the town the visitor can explore the hills by which it is confined to the west and make a number of interesting discoveries. Distances are short and the trip amidst luxuriant, fragrant gardens a great pleasure.

At the foot of one of these hills lies the modest but historic little church of Ag. Georgios ton Philikon containing the icon in front of which those who became members of the Philiki Etairia during the 1821 Revolution swore their allegiance to the cause.

The road now begins to climb up to Strani Hill where a bust of Dionysios Solomos has been erected. This was one of the poet's favourite walks; he would often come up to the hill to enjoy the captivating view over his beloved town, and frequently found inspiration for his verses here in these idyllic surroundings. A little further up the ruins of the fortress that encircled the hill can be seen, remnants of the island's turbulent past.

Perched on the green hillside on the outskirts

of Zakynthos lies the village of Bochali, commanding a breathtaking view over the town and the sea beyond. In this village is the Church of Zoödochos Pigi or Chryssopigi, which contains a Byzantine icon of the Panagia.

Dionysios Romas Street, the road along the sea-front that leads out of town in a northerly direction, passes Kokkinos Vrachos (Red Rock), a well-known spot that was the inspiration for a play by Grigorios Xenopoulos, then Kryoneri Beach and the lighthouse before coming to an end at a beautiful steep promontory covered in greenery.

Viewed from one of the hills that surround it, sunset in the town of Zakynthos is a magic time; it is the moment when the tiled roofs of the houses are bathed in a coppery glow, the last rays of the sun flickering over the flat concrete roofs and caressing the white and ochre walls before sinking into the waters of the harbour and plunging the town into peaceful expectancy of the evening that is approaching.

Sunset on Zakynthos.

THE ISLAND

There are a number of roads which lead out of Zakynthos town heading for the island's interior, with its pretty villages, rustic little houses and lush gardens, and above all the peace and fragrance of the countryside.

Away from the tourist traffic, villages in the interior of the island have managed to retain a remarkable authenticity and genuine traditional character. Visitors to the area are usually only passing through, stopping merely to

Porto Vromi.

admire a historic church or an attractive little chapel, quench their thirst at a village spring or enjoy a cup of Greek coffee with the villagers in a shady café before going on their way.

In the southern part of the island such villages include Ambelokipi, situated amid rich vineyards, Lithakia with Agalas to the west in the foothills of Mount Vrachionas, Pantokratoras, Mouzaki, Romiri and Lagopodo. Continuing along the road into the heart of the island the visitor arrives at Machairado, a pretty village famous for its church of Agia

Mavra, with an icon of the saint that is believed to work miracles. The interior of the church is richly decorated, and has interesting architectural features and an unusual bell-tower. Crowds of people gather here at the beginning of June to celebrate the saint's name-day.

As the road traverses the main part of the island from south to north it passes through several island villages that are quite overgrown with rich vegetation: Melnado, where parts of an ancient temple dedicated to Artemis were found beside the church of Ag. Dimitrios, Bougiato, Langadakia, Fiolitis, Ag. Pantes, Megalo Galero and Ag. Marina (formerly called Fagia). The church of Agia Marina, a three-aisled basilica, is famous for its Baroque wood-carved iconostasis, one of the best of its kind on the island. Its feast-day is celebrated on 17th July.

We have now reached the middle of the island. The road which leads away to the west passes through several mountain villages perched on the slopes of Mount Vrachionas which have magnificent views, lush vegetation and cool springs; for example, Agios Nikolaos, Agios Leon and Kampi, on the west coast, and up in the mountains Loucha and Gyri (at 550 m. the highest village on the island).

To the north-west lies Mariès, with its church dedicated to Mary Magdalene, while still further along the road is the village of Anafonitria, at whose entrance stands a stout rectangular gate which was erected to defend the place from pirate raids. The monastery where Agios Dionysios lived is situated just outside the village. In the cell which he occupied the saint's books are preserved along with a painting showing him granting forgiveness to his brother's murderer. The monastery church has a wonderful wood-carved iconostasis embellished with gold leaf and some not very

The Anafonitria Monastery where St. Dionysios went into retreat.

121

well preserved wall paintings dating from the 17th century. The most valuable icon in the church is a 15th century Byzantine representation of the Panagia. Tradition has it that the icon was brought to the monastery from Constantinople after the city fell to the Turks in 1453. The monastery was to suffer slight damage in the earthquakes.

Not far from Anafonitria Monastery, amid dense pine forest, is the monastery of Agios Georgios at Krimma which commands a fantastic view out over the sea. There is a circular tower here that was erected as a lookout point to guard the area. It is not known when the monastery was built, but there is evidence to show that it was destroyed by pirates in 1553 and the church rebuilt in Venetian style in the 17th century with an opulently decorated ceiling and remarkable iconostasis.

Some picturesque villages lying slightly inland from the island's east coast are Sarakinado, Ag. Kirykos, Kalipado with its church of Ag. Ioannis containing some fine wall paintings, Tragaki, Kypseli with its abundant supply of springs, and Katastari with the monastery of Ag. Ioannis of Langada not far away.

The road now winds its way up to the most northerly point of the island, passing on its way the villages of Orthoniès and Volimes. The 15th century Monastery of Spilaiotissa is to be found near Orthoniès. Volimes is in effect three villages - Ano, Kato and Meses Volimes (Upper, Lower and Middle Volimes). Meses Volimes is the most important of the three settlements and has a beautiful Venetian Baroque church dedicated to Agia Paraskevi. It contains a wood-carved iconostasis with gold veneer and its bell-tower is similar to that of the church of Agios Dionysios in Zakynthos town.

In the same area near the hamlet of Skinaria is the coastal cave at Xyngia, from the depths

Above:
Skinari cape.

Below:
Impressive eliffs and marine grottos.

of which a spring of whitish water that smells strongly of sulphur gushes into the sea.

A rough track now leads to the northernmost tip of the island, Cape Skinari, where the powerful beam from the light-house flashes on and off at regular intervals to guide passing ships away from danger.

On the coast a little to the south of this promontory, at Aspros Vrachos (White Rock) of Krimmos, is the famous Blue Grotto. The entrance to this cave, which was discovered in 1897 and consists of two interconnected chambers, is 6 metres wide and 3.5 metres high. The amazing hue of the bright blue water in the cave is quite breathtaking and the viewer has the feeling that the phosphores-

cent colour is reflected from under the water. The Blue Grotto is one of the island's most impressive sights.

Trips by fishing boat to the Blue Grotto and Xyngia Cave are arranged from Alykes Beach.

THE COAST OF ZAKYNTHOS

In order to explore the island's southern coast the visitor should follow the road out of Zakynthos town towards Argasi, a pretty little seaside village with a beautiful stretch of sandy beach. The church of Ag. Charalambos, built in 1729 and containing an impressive iconostasis as well as several valuable icons, is worth a visit.

Argasi. An attractive seaside village with a beautiful beach.

The road continues to wind in a southerly direction towards Cape Gerakas across a section of the island that juts out like a foot, passing on its way through Xirokastello, Vassilikos and Porto Roma, small hamlets nestling in neat little bays with golden sand and greenery that stretches right down to the water's edge.

The little peninsula is dominated by the tree-covered slopes of Mount Skopos, at the top of which, at a height of 483 metres, is the Monastery of Panagia Skopiotissa. According to archaeologists, the monastery was built around 1400 A.D. out of materials obtained from the ruins of the ancient temple to the goddess Artemis that existed in the area, and was restored after the 1953 earthquakes. It is one of the oldest monasteries on the island. The monastery church is a vaulted, cruciform building in Byzantine style, and contains a number of fine wall paintings.

Another road leading southwards out of Zakynthos town passes through the village of Kalamaki, 5 km. from the town, which has a beautiful sandy beach, and eventually ends up at the 9 km. long beach at Laganas, where there are many tourist installations, restaurants, tavernas, night-clubs and facilities for water sports. From here the visitor can take a boat trip to one of the nearby islands in Laganas Bay - Pelouzo, Agios Sostis, and Marathonissi. On the last of these there are some interesting caves, access to which can be gained from the beach. These little islands are completely unspoiled and the visitor is aware of a pleasant feeling of primitiveness that contrasts sharply with the crowded Laganas Beach.

After Laganas the road turns inland towards Lithakia where it divides, one branch leading in a southerly direction to the lake at Keri, famous since ancient times for its bituminous springs which are mentioned by Herodotus and Pliny. The village of Keri is situated high up on a hill in idyllic surroundings with lush

Above:
The long
beach of
Laganas.

Below: Keri
lake.

vegetation. Its Renaissance-style Church of Panagia Keriotissa, dedicated to the Assumption of the Virgin Mary, has some fine columns at its entrance and contains a marvellous iconostasis.

The outlook from Cape Keri over the rock-studded sea is most impressive, and sunset viewed from this lonely promontory with its lighthouse flashing tirelessly on and off is an unforgettable experience.

The western shore of Zakynthos is inhospitable and the rocky mass of Mount Vrachionas makes access virtually impossible. The road network in this part of the island is almost non-existent and the best way to see the coast is from one of the small boats that make trips around the island. These little caïques skirt the island at a short distance from the shore to enable their passengers to gain some impression of this almost inaccessible side of Zakynthos, passing on their way the islets of Korakonissi and Agios Ioannis, Exo Chora Bay and Vroma Bay and circumnavigating Cape Plemonari not far from Anafonitria Monastery and Agathaki.

The eastern shores of Zakynthos are as popular as those on the south side of the island. The road that leads northwards out of Zakynthos town passes through the picturesque little village of Akrotiri and alongside the organised beach at Kryoneri before going on to Tsilivi and the village of Planos with its luxuriant vineyards, olive groves and orchards of apple and pear trees. This is a popular area for tourists, with a number of facilities and an organised beach. Opposite Tsilivi beach is the little islet of Vodi.

After passing through the village of Planos the road heads away from the coast and up towards the northern part of the island, forking off to the right at Alikanas, a charming little seaside village, and Alykes, nestling inside Alykes Bay. This village owes its name to the

Above:
Alikanas.

Below:
Kalamaki.

nearby saltmarshes from where salt is obtained, and its beach is one of the longest and best-known on the island. There is another popular beach not far away, at Agia Kyriaki.

At Ano Volimes the road forks away to the northeast, passing through the villages of Skinaria and ending up at a small bay to the north of Xyngia Cave. Further north still, lying offshore from a picturesque little cove whose crystal waters are excellent for swimming, is the barren islet of Agios Nikolaos. Not far inland is the village of Korithi, the most northerly settlement on the island from where a road leads down to the Blue Grotto and Cape Skinari.

The beauty of Zakynthos is inexhaustible and the surprises it has in store for the visitor seemingly endless. It is an island of sharp contrasts: the superb caves, full of mystery and magic, its quiet sandy bays, magnificent rock formations, densely forested mountains, fragrant gardens and orchards and verdant plains all contribute to the special and varied character of Zakynthos.

This lovely island was chosen by the rare species of turtle *Caretta caretta* as a place to lay its eggs; the south-coast beaches of Laganas, Kalamaki, Vassilikos, Daphne and Sekania and the islets of Marathonissi and Pelouzo have been designated as biotopes, and large public notice-boards provide the visitor with information about the special measures taken to protect these areas. Local residents, official bodies and ecological organisations are highly sensitive to the threat to the turtle and are collaborating to ensure the survival of this rare animal which visits the shores of Zakynthos to lay its eggs in the warm sand.

The rare Caretta-Caretta turtle.

HOW TO GET TO THE ISLAND

By air from Athens

There are regular daily flights to Zakynthos from Athens via Cephalonia - more frequent in the summer, less so in the winter.
Flight time approximately 45 minutes.

Zakynthos airport is situated at a distance of 4 kilometres from the town. Passengers can take the Olympic Airways bus or a taxi.

Information
* Olympic Airways (OA) - Zakynthos airport: tel.no. 0695/28.322
* Olympic Airways office in Zakynthos town, 16 Al. Roma street.
Reservations: 28.611 and 22.617.

By bus and car ferry from Athens

There are daily bus services (Zakynthos bus service - KTEL) from Athens to the port of Kyllini, on the northwestern coast of the Peloponnese. Departures from the KTEL bus station, 100 Kifissou street, Athens.
The distance from Athens to Kyllini is 286 kilometres, and the journey takes about four and a half hours. From Kyllini there is a direct link by car ferry to Zakynthos. Distance: 18 nautical miles, duration of crossing one and a half hours.

Information
* Athens: KTEL bus station, 100 Kifissou street, tel.01/512.94.32
* Zakynthos: Zakynthos KTEL bus station, tel. 22.656

* Kyllini Harbourmaster's office, tel. 0623/92.211
* Zakynthos Harbourmaster's office, tel. 0695/22.417

By train and car ferry from Athens

Trains run daily from Athens to Kavasila in the prefecture of Eleia (distance from Kyllini 16 kilometres). From there passengers can take a local train (only during the summer months) or taxi to the port of Kyllini, from where they can board a ferry to Zakynthos (duration of journey from Athens to Kyllini approximately six and a half hours).

Information
* Athens, Greek Rail Organization (OSE), Peloponnese Station, tel. 01/513.16.01
* OSE, Pyrgos Eleias Station, tel. 0621/22.576.

HOW TO GET AROUND ON THE ISLAND

By bus

The local KTEL buses which leave daily from Zakynthos town can take the visitor to the following destinations:
Argasi, Xirokastelo, Vassiliko, Port Roma, Tsilivi, Plano, Orthoniés, Anafonitra, Volimes, Exo Hora, Kambi, Aghios Leon, Aghios Nikolaos, Machairado, Galaro, Gyri, Keri, Agala, Lithakia, Laganas.
Information - Bus schedules:
* Zakynthos KTEL, tel. 22.656.

By caïque

Excursions by caïque to the Blue Grotto, to Alykes, Limni Keriou, Marathonissi, are organized by the tourist agencies operating in Zakynthos.
One can also rent a boat and go round the island, visit remote beaches or the desert islands lying off Zakynthos.

By taxi, rented car or motorbike

A good number of taxis are available on the island.
Information:
Taxi rank, tel. nos. 28.104, 28.655, 28.261, 23.788.
There are also car and motorbike rental agencies, as well as many tourist agencies which organise excursions to all the interesting sites on the island.

WHERE TO STAY

On the island you will find accommodation of all types and categories, to suit every requirement and every pocket.

Hotels range from classes A to E. There are also furnished flats, guest houses, rooms to rent, bungalows, as well as organised camping sites for those who prefer life close to nature. Several of these places operate all year round, while others operate from April to October. During the height of the tourist season (end of June to beginning of September), we recommend that you book early, and in any case before setting off for the island.

Information - Reservations
* Hotels Association of Greece, 24 Stadiou Street, Athens, tel. 323.69.62
(reservations by letter)
TELEX 214269 XEPE GR
TELEFAX :(01)322.54.49.

Also, for information and on the spot reservations only: 2, Stadiou and Karayiorgi Servias Street, off Syntagma Square, tel.:(01)323.71.93

* Association of Zakynthos Hoteliers, tel. (0695)22.779 and 25.505
* Zakynthos Tourist Police, tel.:(0695)22.550
NOTE: At the end of the present chapter containing general information, there is a list of Hotels (A, B, and C class) as well as of organised camping sites.

ENTERTAINMENT - SPORTS AND ACTIVITIES

For those who love the night life, Zakynthos offers quite a few opportunities. In the capital town, as well as in several villages and many tourist areas, the visitor will find discos, pubs, bars playing modern music etc. Those who would rather listen to the melodious Zakynthian songs ("cantades") will find plenty of places in town where they can combine a meal with the enjoyment of the local music, songs and dancing.

There are also several tavernas offering genuine Zakynthian specialities, and other restaurants serving international cuisine. Finally, there are pizza parlours, "ouzeries", places where one can try a variety of delicious titbits, coffee shops and pastry shops - or, if one is in a hurry, there are always the ubiquitous "fast food" restaurants preferred by young people.

Apart from the cinemas, one may choose to see a theatrical performance, especially during the summer months, by touring theatre companies.

There are also artistic and cultural events, concerts, exhibitions and lectures etc.

Information on the cultural activities organised by the Municipality of Zakynthos can be obtained by phoning 25.122 and 23.632.

Certain hotels and organised beaches also offer opportunities for water sports (wind surfing, sailing, water skiing). Also there are beaches where one can rent paddle boats and pedalos.

In town and in the large hotels there are tennis courts (information: tel. 28.077)

There is also a mini-golf course. Those keen on fishing will find good fishing grounds at the Skinari point, at Alykes, the islet of Marathonissi, Keri and the desert islands around.

There is also the possibility for servicing and re-provisioning (water, fuel) private yachts. Information: telephone no. 25.598 or inquire at the Harbourmaster's Office).

WHAT TO BUY -LOCAL GOODS

When you leave, you can take with you some typical Zakynthian product to remind you of your enjoyable holiday: cologne made from the sweet-smelling flowers of the Zakynthian countryside, delicious cheeses from the villages of the inland areas, local wine, large, sweet onions, the local sweet called "mandolato" (nougat) made with roasted almonds, etc.

FROM ZAKYNTHOS
TO OTHER DESTINATIONS

Zakynthos is linked by car ferry to:
* Mytikas on mainland Greece (prefecture of Aetoloakarnania), only during the summer months.

* The islands of the Ionian Sea: Lefkas (Nydri), and Cephalonia (Pesada).
Information - Schedules:
Zakynthos Harbourmaster's Office, tel.: 22.417 and 23.566.

NEARBY DESERT ISLANDS

Strophades: This is a group of desert islands which is situated at a distance of 42 nautical miles off the south coast of Zakynthos. On the largest of these is built the impressive 13th century castle-monastery of the Tranfiguration, which is dedicated to the memory of the patron-saint of Zakynthos, Saint Dionysios.

Aghios Ioannis: At a short distance from Zakynthos and oposite the village of Mariés on the west coast, this island is easily accessible.

Plemonari: Very near the beach of the Anafonitria, this island lies off the west coast of Zakynthos.

Aghios Nikolaos: Opposite the north-eastern coast of Zakynthos.

Marathonissi: In the bay of Laganas, opposite Lake Keri.

Pelouzo: This island also is in the bay of Laganas, opposite the village of Vassilikos.

NOTE: These islands can be visited by private or rented boat or by joining an organised excursion.

ACCOMODATION

HOTELS

CLASS	NAME	TEL.	BEDS	CLASS	NAME	TEL.	BEDS
ZAKYNTHOS (TOWN) (0695)				C	COMMODORE	26163	141
A	DIANA PALACE	23070	158	C	FAMILY INN	25359	69
B(H.B.)	ALBA	26641/2	24	C	GAZEBO INN	42300	39
B	LINA	28531	108	C	KRINAS	23566	107
B	STRADA MARINA	22761/3	195	C	LEVANTE	22833	120
B	XENIA	22232	78	C	LOCANDA	25563/4	48
C	ADRIANA	28149	18	C	MIRABELLE	26435	51
C	AEGLI	28317	16				
C	ANGELICA	22391	32	**BOCHALI** (0661)			
C	APOLLON	42838	17	B	VARRES	28352	67
C	BIZZARO	23644	74	B(FF.)	ZANTE PALACE	26150	61
C	DIANA	28547	91	C	AKROTIRI	28000	31
C(F.F)	GARDELINO	44333	40		LOFOS STRANI		50
C	KRYONERI	28000	27				
C	PALATINO	27780/2	49	**GAITANI** (0695)			
C	PHOENIX	42419	65	C	PARK	23790	140
C	PLAZA	48909	37				
C	REPARO	23578	28	**KALAMAKI** (0695)			
C	SALVOS	176	32001	B	BIZZARO PALACE	23935	169
C	YRIA	44682/3	26	B	CLELIA	27056	86
				B	CHRYSSOS ILIOS	-	82
AGRILIA (0695)				B	EXOTICA	27740	112
C	AGRILIA	51745	7	B	KALAMAKI BEACH	22575	55
				B	MARLENE	26137/41	32
ALIKANAS (0661)				B	SIROCCO	26083/6	67
B	VALAIS	83223	5	B(FF.)	VANESSA	26713	47
C	KALI PIGHI	83075	68	B	VENUS	27459	52
C(FF.)	VILLA SANTA MONICA	83550	29	C	CAVO DORO	22451	124
				C	CRYSTAL SEA	22917	108
ALYKES (0695)				C	DANIEL	26094/6	26
A(FF.)	ALYKES PAPK	83592	48	C	DENIS INN	27785	77
C	CONSTANTINOS	83061	65	C	LOUROS BEACH	23025	54
				C	METAXA	27441/3	62
ARGASI (0695)				C(B)	RANIA		48
A	AKTI ZAKANTHA	26441/3	220	C	YIANNIS & ZOE	27794	57
A	KATERINA PALACE	26998	123				
B	CHRYSSI AKTI	28679	146	**KATASTARI** (0695)			
B	CONTESSA	25152	150	C	ASTORIA	83533	64
B	ELEANA		59	C	IONIAN STAR	83416	42
B(B)	MIMOSA BEACH	22588	13	C	MONTREAL	83241	56
B	PALMYRA	25707	129				
B	PARADISE BEACH	69		**LAGANAS** (0695)			
B	YLIESSA	25346	133	A	ZANTE PARK	51948/9	196
C	ADMIRAL	42779	192	B	ASTIR	51730/3	158
C	ARGASI BEACH	28554	71	B	CALIFORNIA BEACH	51392	115
C	CAPTAIN'S	22779	69	B	ESPERIA	51505/7	62
C(FF.)	CASTELLO	23520	152	B	GALAXY	51171/3	152

ACCOMODATION

HOTELS

CLASS	NAME	TEL.	BEDS	CLASS	NAME	TEL.	BEDS
B	IKAROS		99	C	DIAS	28105	85
B	LAGANAS	51793/6	91	C	ORAIA ELENI	28788	52
B	PALACE	51805	46	C	PARADEISOS	25096	27
B	POSEIDON BEACH	51199	276	C	TERESA	24500	5
B(H.B.)	ZANTE BEACH	51130	494	C	TSILIVI	23109	105
B	ZANTE HOTEL	51611	74				
C	ALKYONIS	51194	58	**ROGHIA** (0695)			
C	AUSTRALIA	51071/3	45	A	ROGHIA	61659	57
C	BLUE COAST	22287	20				
C	BYZANTION	51136	16	**TRAGAKI** (0695)			
C	CASTELLI	52367/9	58	A	CARAVEL II	25261/5	138
C	ELLINIS	51164	17				
C	EUGENIA	51149	24	**VASSILIKOS** (0695)			
C(FF.)	GALAZIA KYMATA	51791	50	A	GOLDEN BAYI VILLAGE	35435/8	183
G	I HARA TIS THALASSAS			B	AQUARIUS	35300/2	46
C	IONIS	51141	91	B	MATILDA	35376	61
C	MARGARITA	51534	106	C	VASSILIKON BEACH	24114	60
C	MEGAS ALEXANDROS	51580/3	245				
C	OLYMPIA	51644	80	**VOLIMES** (0695)			
C	PANORAMA	51144	26	B	BLUE CAVE	27013	76
C	PARASKEVI		39	C	LA GROTTA	31224	29
C	PERCHE		81				
C	SELENE	51154	24				
C	SIREN	51188	58				
C	SISSY	52266/7	48				
C	VESSAL	51155	16				
C	VICTORIA	51617	266				

CLASS	NAME	TEL.	BEDS
LITHAKIA (0695)			
B	PORTO KOUKLA	51577	54
C	BOZIKIS PALACE	51563	56
MOUZAKI (0695)			
B	OSCAR	51990	70
C(FF.)	PORTEGO		50
PANTOCRATORAS (0695)			
C	ARCHONTIKO YIANNAKOU	1940	26
PLANOS (TSILIVI) (O695)			
A(FF.)	SAINT DENIS	25296/8	48
B	MAVRIKOS	25907	72
B	MEDITERRANEE	26101	76
C	ALEXANDRA BEACH	26190	104
C	ANETIS	24590	23
C	COSMOPOLITE	28752	27

NOTES:
* *There are also D- and E-class hotels and rooms to let. Information: Zakynthos Tourist Police.*
* *The information regarding the hotels in our list have been taken from the publication of the Hotels Association of Greece entitled Greek Hotels 1995.*
* *H = hotel*
* *B = bungalows*
* *P = Pension*
* *FF= Furnished Flats*

CAMPING SITES

LAGANAS (Laganas) τηλ: 51.585
PARADEISOS (Meso Gerakari) τηλ: 61.888
TARTARUGA (Lithakia) τηλ: 51.417
ZANTE (Tragaki) τηλ: 44.754, 61.710

NOTE :
The camping sites are in operation from April to October.

USEFUL TELEPHONE NUMBERS

Zakynthos Automatic Dialling Code:.........0695
Zakynthos Police: 22.100
Tourist Police: 22.550
Municipality: 22.315
Telecommunications (OTE): 22.139
Post Office (ELTA): 22.418
General Hospital: 22.514/5
Volimes Rural Clinic: 31.201
Kalipados Rural Clinic:........................... 61.301
Katastari Rural Clinic: 83.208
Machairado Rural Clinic: 92.217
Pantocrator Rural Clinic: 51.210
Post-Byzantine Museum: 22.714
Mausoleum of the poets
Solomos and Kalvos and other
eminent Zakynthians: 28.982
Municipal Library- Art Gallery and
Zakynthos Historical Archives:...............28.128

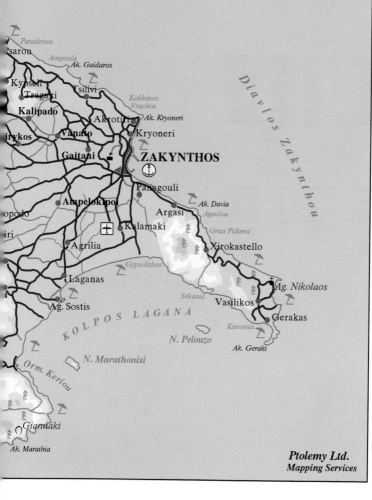

. ZAKYNTHOS

Scale 1 : 200.000

Paradeisos
sarou
Ampoula
Kyps
Ak. Gaidaros
Tragaki
Tsilivi
Kalipado
Kokkinos
Vrachos
Akrotiri
Ak. Kryoneri
rykos
Vanato
Kryoneri
Gaitani
ZAKYNTHOS

Panagouli
opodo
Ampelokipol
Argasi
Ak. Davia
Agoulou
iri
Kalamaki
Grias Pidima
Agrilia
Xirokastello
Gypsolithos
Laganas
Sekania
Ag. Nikolaos
Ag. Sostis
Vasilikos
KOLPOS LAGANA
Kanonia
Gerakas
N. Pelouzo
Ak. Geraki
N. Marathonisi
Orm. Keriou
Giannaki
Ak. Marathia

Diavlos Zakynthou

Ptolemy Ltd.
Mapping Services

TEXT: ELENI PALASKA - PAPASTATHI

FOTOS: K. ADAM - G. VACHARIDIS
              A. RODOPOULOS - K. MITRELIS
              G. KOUROUPIS

PRINT: PERGAMOS ABEE